An Unauthorized
Biography

HIP-HOP
MOGULS

Eminem
Hip-Hop Mogul

Jeff Burlingame

Speeding Star
Keep Boys Reading!

Library of Congress Cataloging-in-Publication Data

Burlingame, Jeff, author.
    Eminem : hip-hop mogul / Jeff Burlingame.
        pages cm. — (Hip-hop moguls)
    Includes bibliographical references and index.
    Summary: "In this biography of Hip-Hop mogul Eminem, learn everything from his early
        childhood struggles in Detroit to his controversial lyrics that have made him one of the best-
        selling artists of all-time"— Provided by publisher.
    ISBN 978-1-62285-206-2
    1. Eminem, 1972—Juvenile literature. 2. Rap musicians—United States—Biography—
    Juvenile literature. I. Title.
    ML3930.E46B87 2014
    782.421649092—dc23
        [B]   2013044975

Future Editions:
Paperback ISBN: 978-1-62285-207-9   EPUB ISBN: 978-1-62285-208-6
Single-User PDF ISBN: 978-1-62285-209-3   Multi-User PDF: 978-1-62285-210-9

Printed in the United States of America
052014 Lake Book Manufacturing, Inc., Melrose Park, IL
10 9 8 7 6 5 4 3 2 1

To Our Readers: This book has not been authorized by Eminem or his agents.

We have done our best to make sure all Internet addresses in this book were active and
appropriate when we went to press. However, the author and the Publisher have no control
over, and assume no liability for, the material available on those Internet sites or on other Web
sites they may link to. Any comments or suggestions can be sent by e-mail to comments@
speedingstar.com or to the address below:

Speeding Star
Box 398, 40 Industrial Road
Berkeley Heights, NJ 07922
USA
www.speedingstar.com

Illustration Credits: ©AP Images/Carlos Osorio, pp. 21, 33; ©AP Images/Chris Pizzello, p.
30; ©AP Images/Damian Dovarganes, p. 6; ©AP Images/Jason DeCrow, p. 39; ©AP Images/
Kevork Djansezian, pp. 8, 9, 10; ©AP Images/Matt Sayles, pp. 40, 42; ©AP Images/Paul
Sancya, p. 29; ©AP Images/PRNewsFoto/Interscope Records, p. 13; ©AP Images/Ramin
Talaie, p. 36; ©AP Images/Rob Widdis, p. 27; ©AP Images/Ron Frehm, p. 23; Wikipedia.com
Public Domain Image/Photographer Tim Kiser, p. 13/ Wikipedia.com Public Domain image/
Photographer WacoJacko, p. 17.

Cover Illustration: ©AP Images/Matt Sayles

Contents

Each year, America's best musical acts gather in Los Angeles for the Grammy Awards, an over-the-top ceremony where winners are selected in dozens of categories. The Grammys are the country's biggest musical event of the year: Millions of people watch the awards on TV, not only to find out who won, but also to see some of their favorite stars perform on stage. That fact puts a lot of pressure on the stars that perform there. They must make their few minutes on stage memorable.

Chapter 1

The Hug Heard 'Round the World

Sometimes, that can mean a performance so touching that those viewing are brought to tears. Other times, it can mean a routine so bizarre that people talk about it for days afterward.

Some of the best-known musicians of all time have performed under the bright lights of the Grammys. In 1988, "King of Pop" Michael Jackson moved the audience to tears with his performance of "Man in the Mirror." One year later, legendary singer Whitney Houston did the same with her inspirational song, "One Moment in Time." Jackson's and Houston's performances are considered among the best in the storied history of the

Shown before the start of the Grammy Awards, GLAAD and their advocates made it known that they were not okay with Eminem being recognized positively for his lyrics.

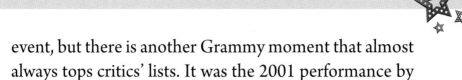

event, but there is another Grammy moment that almost always tops critics' lists. It was the 2001 performance by rapper Eminem.

That show took place February 21 at L.A.'s Staples Center. The crowd that night was full of celebrities and the lineup full of star performers, but Eminem is the one that a majority of Americans tuned in to see. The Detroit rapper's third album had been released just a few months earlier and many groups and organizations had taken offense to lyrics on it they deemed offensive. One of those organizations was the Gay & Lesbian Alliance Against Defamation (GLAAD), which felt many of Eminem's lyrics were homophobic. Weeks before the 2001 Grammys, GLAAD announced it would stage a protest outside the Staples Center on the day of the event. Several other organizations joined in. GLAAD's entertainment director, Scott Seomin, said at the time: "[Eminem's] lyrics encourage violence against gays and lesbians and women," and that the rapper's lyrics were hateful and derogatory.

By that time, it was well known that Eminem had planned to use his Grammy moment to fire back at GLAAD. Weeks earlier, Eminem had announced that superstar entertainer Elton John, a gay man and a longtime activist for gay rights, was going to join him on stage to sing the song "Stan." GLAAD was furious at John's decision to team with Eminem. The group had sent a letter to John asking him to reconsider his decision to sing with Eminem. When that did not stop him, the

group spoke out publicly. "We feel betrayed by Elton John, who has used his gayness for good and here he's using it for evil," Seomin said.

John defended his decision in the media. He told *The Los Angeles Times*: "I'm a big fan of [Eminem's] music, and I said I would be delighted to [do the song]. I know I'm going to get a lot of flak from various people

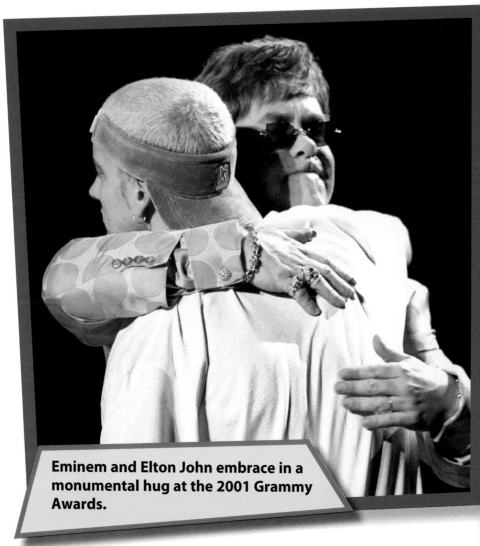

Eminem and Elton John embrace in a monumental hug at the 2001 Grammy Awards.

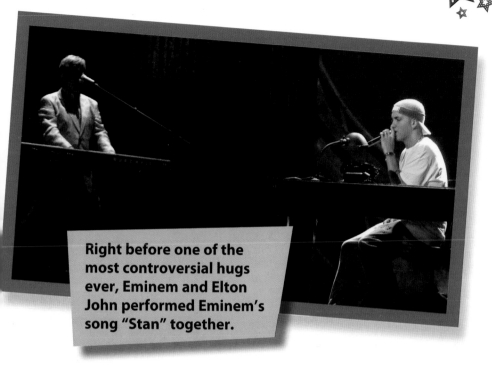

Right before one of the most controversial hugs ever, Eminem and Elton John performed Eminem's song "Stan" together.

who are going to picket the show. [But} I'd rather tear down walls between people than build them up. If I thought for one minute that he was [hateful], I wouldn't do it."

Eminem and John did do it, taking to the stage—set up to look like a bedroom with a large video screen in the background displaying a lightning storm—for nearly six-and-a-half minutes. After the song was finished, Eminem and John met in the middle of the stage and hugged each other. *Entertainment Weekly* said: "It was the hug heard 'round the world."

In a book he wrote years later, Eminem also said he knew how important that moment on stage was: "My performance with Elton John … that was history. … Elton put himself at risk by performing with me—in terms of

Even after all the controversy, Eminem still won three Grammys in 2001.

alienating his fans who had a problem with me—and I'll always respect him for that. The gesture helped immensely, and it made me not sweat the fact that there were all those protesters outside wanting me to go away forever."

For Eminem, the notorious Grammy performance and the controversy that surrounded it was just another day on the job. The twenty-eight-year-old, blue-eyed rapper had grown used to being in the spotlight. He knew many people hated him. He knew many people loved him. But the most surprising facet of Eminem's life was the fact that anyone knew who he was at all.

The odds said success probably would not be in the cards for Marshall Bruce Mathers III when he was born October 17, 1972, in St. Joseph, a mid-sized city in northwestern Missouri best known for being the place where legendary outlaw Jesse James took his final breath after being shot by a trusted member of his gang in 1882.

When Marshall III was born, his "gang" was only three members large. His mother, Debbie, was just seventeen years old. For two years, she had been married to Marshall's father,

Chapter 2

8 Mile Road

Marshall Mathers II. Marshall II had been twenty-two years old when he and Debbie had married, and twenty-four years old when his first son was born.

Marshall II's job soon pulled the young family to North Dakota. There, Marshall II and his wife Debbie performed at various hotels in the region in a band

Eminem was born in St. Joseph, Missouri.
This is a view of downtown taken in 2006.

13

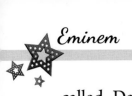

called Daddy Warbucks. Neither the band, nor the relationship, lasted long. The Mathers separated in 1974 and divorced the following year. Debbie and her son moved back to Missouri, where she worked various jobs while family members cared for her boy. Marshall II moved to California, leaving his son to grow up without a father. Marshall III would later say he had no memories of his father and had never even seen a picture of him. In Missouri, the boy was mostly cared for by his dad's aunt and uncle, Edna and Charles Swartz. "They took care of me a lot," Marshall told *Rolling Stone* years later. "They were older but they did things with me. They let me stay the weekends there, took me to school, bought me things, let me stay and watch TV, let me cut the grass to get five dollars, took me to the mall. Between them and my Uncle Ronnie, they were my solidity."

Sometimes, when the phone would ring in the Swartz home, Marshall's father would be on the other end of the line. The boy later remembered: "[A] lot of times he'd call, and I'd be there—maybe I'd be on the floor coloring or watching TV—and it wouldn't have been nothing for him to say, 'Put him on the phone.' He coulda talked to me, let me know something..."

Marshall's permanent residences during his earliest years were various public housing projects in Missouri. Yet he and his mother rarely lived in one home longer than a year. That meant Marshall frequently changed schools, which did not prove to be easy on the boy.

By eleven, Marshall had become somewhat of an introvert. That also is when he first took an interest in creating music. It was then that his Uncle Ronnie showed him how to record beats and rap over the top of them by simultaneously using two cassette decks. A tape of one of those recordings, Marshall later wrote in his book, *The Way I Am*, changed the boy's life: "I made a copy and took that tape home and listened to it over and over. That's when I realized I wanted to do it by myself: rap." Marshall began listening to whatever rap music he could get his hands on, and even began break dancing—an activity commonly associated with rap.

Around that time, Marshall's mother again uprooted the family from Missouri. She and her son went to live in and around the bigger city of Detroit, Michigan. In Detroit, Debbie met, and eventually married, a man named Fred Samra, Jr. By all accounts, Marshall initially liked his new stepfather. In 1986, Debbie and Fred had a child together, Nathan, and Marshall formed a close relationship with his half-brother, too. From the outside, life at home appeared to be stable, and in many respects it was. Although, Marshall later would claim his mom had abused prescription drugs throughout his childhood.

At school, short and skinny Marshall often was bullied and beaten by his peers. "[I got] beat up in the bathroom, beat up in hallways, shoved into lockers," he later told *60 Minutes*. In one incident, Marshall was hurt so badly he ended up in the hospital. He later wrote about the incident in a song called "Brain Damage."

Marshall eventually further retreated into himself and turned to hip-hop music for solace. He began drawing and writing poetry and lyrics. His mom later wrote in her book, *My Son Marshall, My Son Eminem,* that "He scribbled lyrics over napkins, scraps of paper, even grocery-store receipts, and he woke me up constantly in the middle of the night to ask what words meant. I bought him a dictionary. He pored over it, memorizing unusual words and meanings."

When Marshall was fifteen, he moved with his family to a small house in Warren, a suburb located near Detroit's 8 Mile Road. He attended high school there, failed the ninth grade three times, and eventually dropped out. It was not because he was stupid, he would later say, but because he could not deal with the difficult circumstances life had handed him—both at school and at home.

By the time he dropped out of school, Marshall was a couple years into a relationship with his first serious girlfriend, a tall blonde named Kim Scott. Marshall had met Kim when he was fifteen years old and she was thirteen. Although she was young, Kim already had lived a difficult life. According to Marshall's mother, Kim "... had no idea who her real father was, and claimed to have been sexually abused by her stepfather... [and] she'd been raped, forced to sleep with relatives on a regular basis, [and] beaten by her mother."

Marshall told *Rolling Stone* he met Kim: "... the day she got out of the youth home. I was at a friend's house,

While Eminem spent time in North Dakota and Missouri during the earliest parts of his childhood, the most important years of his life were spent growing up in 8 Mile.

and his sister was friends with her.... And I'm standing on the table with my shirt off...mocking the words to LL Cool J's "I'm Bad." And I turn around and she's at the door.... She's thirteen, she's taller than me, and she didn't look that young."

At seventeen and still dating Kim, Marshall took a job as a cook at a family restaurant called Gilbert's Lodge in Detroit. Marshall later told *NY Rock*: "When I was just working in Gilbert's Lodge, everything was moving in slow motion." For several reasons, Marshall's life was about to speed up. And no one had a clue just how fast it would become.

arshall's best friend growing up was DeShaun Holton, a slightly older African-American kid Marshall met when he was fourteen. Marshall and Holton—who was known in the neighborhood by his nickname "Proof"—had a lot in common. Both boys came from broken homes, both had musical parents, and both loved rapping and hip-hop music. By the time he and Proof met, Marshall already had spent a great deal of time doing both.

Marshall's musical exploits took place at

Chapter 3

Braggin' and Boasting

the home of former classmate Mike "Manix" Ruby. Ruby had a recording studio in the basement of his parents' home, and he and Marshall would spend hours recording songs there. It was in that basement that Marshall developed a stage name based on his initials. He decided he would call himself "M&M." Later, he would change the spelling of his stage name to "Eminem."

Eminem, Proof, and Ruby—as well as Ruby's twin brother, Matt—spent most of their free time trying to make it as rappers. They were mildly successful at doing so. At the time, the Detroit hip-hop scene, like the national hip-hop scene, was dominated by black performers. Proof was black, but Ruby and Eminem were white. Eminem knew that, as a white rapper, it would be difficult for him to be taken seriously. If he wanted to perform his raps in public, Eminem believed, he would have to get good at battling.

Battling, in the hip-hop world, meant going one-on-one onstage or elsewhere with another rapper. The two battlers would take turns rapping insults at one another set to music in front of a crowd. The winner and loser were determined either by the crowd's reaction or a panel of judges.

Many of Eminem's earliest battles took place at The Hip Hop Shop, a Detroit venue mostly frequented by African Americans. It proved to be a difficult crowd for him to win over, and he was not successful at his earliest battles. "As soon as I grabbed the mike, I'd get booed," he told *Rolling Stone* in 1999.

inem persevered. He joined several rap groups with Proof and others. He improved his rapping, became somewhat vicious in his attacks on whomever he was battling, and perfected a style of rapping that was fairly unique at the time. In his raps, Eminem made a conscious effort to not only make sure the end of each line rhymed, as was typical, but also that there were rhymes within the lines themselves. Soon, crowds were coming to see the "white boy" they once had dissed.

Eminem gained confidence in his abilities. In 2010, he told *60 Minutes*: "Hip-hop has always been braggin' and boasting and 'I'm better at you than this' and 'I'm better at you than that.' And I finally found something that yeah, this kid over here, you know, he may have more chicks, and he may, you know, have better clothes, or whatever, but he can't do this like me. You know what I mean? He can't write what I'm writing right now. And it started to feel like, you know, maybe Marshall's getting a little respect."

That respect came not only from listeners, but also from those who could help Eminem gain a wider audience. Two such people were brothers Jeff and Mark Bass, who owned an independent record label and a small studio they called the Bassmint. "[Eminem] was phenomenal," Mark Bass told *Salon* in 2000. "I dropped everything I was doing and I put everything I had into this kid."

At the time, circa 1995, the twenty-three-year-old "kid" had a lot going on in his personal life, too. During

Growing up, Eminem and DeShaun Holton, or Proof, became best friends and remained that way until Proof's death in 2006.

an "on" period in his on-again, off-again relationship with Kim Scott, he had gotten her pregnant. Eminem's first daughter, Hailie Jade Scott, was born December 25, 1995. Eminem later said he did not want Hailie to grow up without a father like he did: "I know and I want to be there for my daughter, whenever she needs me. I want to be with her on every step of the way, ya know. She's the best thing that happened to me."

With the help of the Bass brothers, Eminem appeared to be a on a path where one day rapping might even pay the bills and allow him to provide for his daughter. Less than a year after Hailie was born, Eminem

released his first album on Mark and Jeff Bass' local label. The album was called *Infinite*.

Many who listened to the eleven-track, thirty-eight-minute effort believed it lacked direction. They called it watered-down rap that showed off Eminem's talents as a DJ but did not offer much that was unique or powerful enough for listeners to grab hold of. Hardly anyone bought *Infinite*. Radio stations did not play its songs. Critics told Eminem he could not be a rapper because he was white. Even Eminem later said he was not fond of the way *Infinite* turned out. He told *Rolling Stone*: "It was [recorded] right before my daughter was born, so having a future for her was all I talked about. It was way hip-hopped out, like Nas and AZ—that rhyme style that was real in at the time. I've always been a smart-ass comedian, and that's why it wasn't a good album."

The commercial failure of *Infinite* marked the beginning of another rough patch in Eminem's life. After he and Kim broke up that same year, Eminem began using drugs and alcohol more than ever. He even tried to kill himself by overdosing on Tylenol. Though the suicide attempt failed, it was clear to everyone around him that Eminem was depressed. He later wrote in his 2008 autobiography: "Rap was always a pipe dream for me, but rap was all that I had. Because really, what was I going to do with my life? I had a young daughter. Kim and I were always either getting evicted or our house was getting shot up or robbed."

A few short years after he released *Infinite*, Eminem stormed into the hip-hop world. Soon he was the biggest star there. He even won the MTV Video Music Award for Best New Artist in 1999.

All the negativity in his life made Eminem a negative person. Though it seems counterintuitive, being negative actually helped Eminem's career. After he traveled to Los Angeles to compete in the Rap Olympics—where he lost in the finals—Eminem returned to Detroit and channeled his negativity into creating an alter ego that would help launch him to heights most rappers would never reach. Eminem began to dress the part of a white-trash man from Detroit, which essentially he was, and rap with a higher-pitched, whiny voice. He used peroxide to bleach his hair blonde and wrote controversial,

off-the-wall lyrics intended to shock listeners as much as possible, while exploring the darker parts of his life that had left him so depressed. He gave his new persona a name: "Slim Shady."

"Being able to rap as an entirely different persona feels good," Eminem wrote in his 2008 autobiography. "Proof used to describe it like this: Slim Shady is the guy who shows up after a few shots of Bacardi; Eminem is the emcee who goes onstage sober and spits metaphors. Slim Shady gets drunk and wants to fight."

Eminem was quick to get his new persona on tape. He did so in 1997, recording a ten-song album called *The Slim Shady EP*. The record did not sell well, but it did create a buzz in the underground music world. Those who heard *The Slim Shady EP* enjoyed its content. It also led to much bigger things for its creator. While he was departing the Rap Olympics in disgust, Eminem halfheartedly tossed a copy of the recording to some unknown man who asked for one.

Unknown to Eminem at the time, the man who had asked for the recording worked for Interscope Records, a major label that had released music by many superstar musicians. *The Slim Shady EP* eventually ended up in the hand of Interscope's boss, Jimmy Iovine, who played it for legendary musician and producer Dr. Dre. Dr. Dre later told *Rolling Stone*: "In my entire career in the music industry, I have never found anything from a demo tape or a CD. When Jimmy played [*The Slim Shady EP*], I said, 'Find him. Now.'"

D r. Dre found Eminem back in Detroit, and signed the twenty-five-year-old rapper to his label, Aftermath Entertainment. The pair quickly took to the studio to record Eminem's first major-label release. It was called *The Slim Shady LP,* and played up Eminem's new persona to the fullest. Released in February 1999, the twenty-track effort featured songs riddled with anger, dark humor, and violence. Many of the lyrics were rooted in truth but exaggerated for effect. The general

Chapter 4

His Name Is Slim Shady

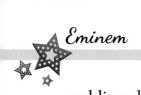

public, which had no idea what parts of what Eminem was saying were fact and what was fiction, was either hot or cold on the rapper from the start.

Professional music critics generally loved the album. Fans of rap music did, too. Within weeks of its release, *The Slim Shady LP* had gone platinum, selling more than one million copies. Songs such as the single "My Name Is" could be heard bumping from car stereos across the country—from California to New York—and Eminem's face soon was all over the covers of major magazines and newspapers, and his videos were in hot rotation on MTV. Seemingly overnight, Eminem had gone from unknown to superstar.

Still, there was plenty of bad to go along with the good of Eminem's newfound success. Most of that bad stemmed from Eminem's lyrics, which talked about murder, rape, and homophobia. Many parents found the lyrics profane and refused to let their children listen to them. Even Eminem's family had problems with what he was rapping. In fact, his mother sued him for $10 million for some of the things he said about her in the media and on his record. On "My Name Is," for example, he talked about how bad of a drug user she was. She denied that claim.

The lawsuit further tore apart what was an already-strained relationship between mother and son. It also further strained the relationship between Eminem and his daughter's mother, Kim. Although Kim and Eminem had gotten married in 1999, their relationship had never been perfect. One of the songs on *The Slim Shady LP*, "'97 Bonnie and Clyde," centered on Eminem and his baby daughter Hailie taking a drive to the beach to dispose of Kim's dead body, which was hidden in the trunk. Eminem defended the song on several occasions, basically saying it was a joke. When *Rolling Stone* asked him what he would tell his daughter when she asked about the song, Eminem said: "When she gets old enough, I'm going to explain it to her. I'll let her know

When Eminem first signed with Dr. Dre, he wanted to give off the look of a real "bad boy" to go along with the theme of his lyrics.

that Mommy and Daddy weren't getting along at the time. None of it was to be taken literally. Although at the time, I wanted to...do it." Shortly after the song's release, Kim attempted suicide by cutting her wrists at home. Her attempt was unsuccessful.

Eminem brought many of his non-music-related troubles upon himself. In June 2000, he was charged with pistol-whipping a man who he said was kissing his wife outside a bar. In another incident the same month, he was arrested for carrying a concealed weapon and displaying it in public.

Such legal and personal troubles seemed to have little impact on Eminem's musical career. He toured the country with several high-profile acts and became a favorite guest of MTV's hit show *Total Request Live*. *The Slim Shady LP* won the Grammy Award for Best Rap Album, and "My Name Is" won a Grammy for Best Solo Rap Performance. Eminem clearly was the hottest rapper in the world. He and Dr. Dre decided to capitalize on that fame and record and release Eminem's second album as quickly as possible.

That album, *The Marshall Mathers LP*, was released in May 2000. In the first week it was available for purchase, it sold nearly 2 million copies. That was more than twice as many records as any other rap artists ever had ever sold in one week. The success of the album had been helped by the earlier release of its popular lead single, "The Real Slim Shady." The song became a top-five hit in the United States, a rare accomplishment for

Eminem has not allowed his run-ins with the law to slow down his music career, nor have they stopped him from writing extremely controversial lyrics.

Eminem had no way of knowing that giving that CD to Jimmy Iovine would change his life forever. He was going to be in the hands of one of hip-hop's founding fathers, Dr. Dre (left).

a rap song. The song's lyrics took aim at what Eminem deemed was ridiculous about pop culture, including the "bubblegum" singers currently topping the charts. The song's lyrics were graphic, yet still somewhat tame by Eminem standards.

The rest of the album was nuanced. Featuring a hook sung by British pop artist Dido, "Stan" took on the topic of a crazed, obsessed fan that placed his pregnant girlfriend in the trunk of his car and drove off a bridge. "The Way I Am" featured Eminem's thoughts on his newfound celebrity, and "Kill You" talked about Eminem raping his mother. Many listeners felt the most shocking song on the album was "Kim." The plot centered on Eminem confronting his wife about an affair he believed she was having, and then abusing her and contemplating killing her, her lover, and her lover's young son. Not surprisingly, Eminem and Kim divorced in 2001. They were awarded joint custody of Hailie, who was five years old at the time.

Advocates for gay rights also had a big problem with Eminem's lyrics, particularly due to his liberal use of the term "faggot," which gays felt was derogatory. Eminem said that, although he frequently used the word, he did not see it as being hateful at all. In his 2008 autobiography, Eminem wrote: "I think it's hard for some people to understand that for me the word 'faggot' has nothing to do with sexual preference. I meant it something more like [jerks]....ultimately, who you choose to be in a relationship with...is your business."

Eminem spent a lot of time defending himself in the media. His basic defense was simple: his lyrics were jokes and written from the perspective of his angry alter ego Slim Shady. No one, he said, should take what he writes seriously. Still, people did. Many people worshipped Eminem; dressing like him and singing his music. Soon the new star began to dislike being so famous. He told *NY Rock*: "I always wished for this, but it's almost turning into more of a nightmare than a dream. I mean, everybody wants to ride on my...coattails....You gotta be careful what you wish for; you just might get it.... I can't go out anymore and play basketball, because everybody knows my...face. All I really wanted was to have a career in hip-hop and now I got to deal with so much [stuff]! There are people coming to my house, knocking on the door. Either they want autographs or they wanna fight. It's...crazy!"

In some ways, Eminem was even guilty of riding on his own coattails. One of the ways he did that was by reforming D12, a group he had been in prior to making it big. D12 had six members, including Eminem and his best friend Proof. Eminem created a record label called Shady Records and signed the band. D12 released a couple albums, including *Devil's Night*, which debuted in June 2001 as the best-selling record in the United States.

In the early 2000s, it was clear to everyone—those who loved Eminem and those who hated him—that everything the rapper touched quickly turned to gold. Or platinum, as was the case of his third major-label

Eminem performs with actor Mekhi Phifer (left) and Proof (middle) in 2003. Phifer starred in *8 Mile.*

release, *The Eminem Show*, which came out in May 2002. Featuring the hit songs "Without Me" and the mother-bashing "Cleanin' Out My Closet," *The Eminem Show* sold nearly 1.5 million copies in its first week. At the 2003 Grammy Awards, the album won an award for Best Rap Album and was even nominated for Album of the Year, an amazing feat for a rap album.

Eminem even ventured off into the acting world. Most notably, he starred in *8 Mile*, a movie based on his life growing up in and around Detroit, and the struggles he faced in trying to become a white rapper in a black-dominated field. The movie's sound track included five songs featuring Eminem. Of those, "Lose Yourself" was the most popular. It won an Academy Award for Best Original Song.

Eminem's influence was widespread. For every person who loved his music, there was another person who simply loved what he represented: that angry, alienated youths of any color in any American city had a chance to succeed or, at the very least, had someone who represented them. Eminem's critics, meanwhile, simply bided their time, waiting for him to fall from grace.

The wrong turn—either in his career or in his personal life—that Eminem's detractors were expecting him to take, did not happen as quickly as many expected. At the end of 2004, Eminem's fourth major-label album, *Encore*, was released and sold roughly 1.5 million copies in the first two weeks it was available.

Encore was a bit mellower than its predecessors, but its songs still managed to created controversy. Tracks on the recording attacked everything from Eminem's ex-wife

Chapter 5

Crashing and Crying

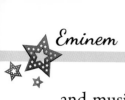
and music legend Michael Jackson, to the president of the United States.

Although highly successful—the album earned three Grammy nominations—*Encore* marked the beginning of Eminem's lengthy hiatus from recording music. One reason for this was that Eminem the rapper had become Eminem the business mogul. Other ventures—some music-related, some not—now were occupying most of his time. Eminem started a hip-hop-centric satellite radio station called Shade 45 and also started his own urban clothing line, Shady Ltd. He continued to run

Eminem appears at the Roseland Ballroom for The Shady National Convention concert where his Sirius station (now called Sirius XM), Shade 45, was launched.

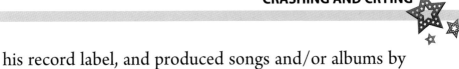

his record label, and produced songs and/or albums by superstars such as Jay-Z, Nas, and 50 Cent. He was busy, but not necessarily creating his own music.

Eminem's home life had changed dramatically by the time *Encore* was released. His ex-wife, Kim, had been arrested several times on drug-related charges and had spent time in jail. This had left Eminem with the responsibility of caring for Hailie. It was a job he took seriously. In 2004, he told *Rolling Stone*: "It's no secret what's been going on over the past year with my ex-wife. I wouldn't down-talk her, but with her being on the run from the cops I really had no choice but to just step up to the plate."

Eminem also had stepped up to the plate to care for two other children. He had long had full custody of his niece, Alaina, and for years he had been caring for his younger half-brother, Nathan, who years earlier had been taken away from his mother by the state and placed in a foster home.

Eminem's ex-wife was not the only one dealing with a drug problem. When a large portion of Eminem's 2005 world tour was canceled so he could check himself into rehab, it became public that the rapper had a problem with drugs, too. Eminem's drugs of choice were prescription ones. He had become addicted to Ambien, Valium, and Vicodin. Eminem said he first began taking the drugs to help him sleep. Then, he told *Rolling Stone*, "I was taking so many pills that I wasn't even taking them to get high anymore. I was taking them to feel normal.

Not that I didn't get high. I just had to take a ridiculous amount. I want to say in a day I could consume anywhere from 40 to 60 Valium. And Vicodin...maybe 20, 30? I don't know."

The always-skinny Eminem gained a lot of weight during the period. He even remarried, then quickly re-divorced, his childhood girlfriend, Kim. He later said that the 2006 murder of his childhood friend Proof had a lot to do with him not being able to quit using drugs. He told *Rolling Stone*: "I remember days I spent just taking …pills and crying. One day, I couldn't get out of bed. I didn't even want to get up to use the bathroom."

Eminem's drug issues came to a head in 2007. That December, he overdosed on methadone, a narcotic often used to help heroin addicts. All Eminem remembered of the incident was that he went to bed one day after taking the drug, then he woke up in the hospital. He told *Rolling Stone*: "The first thing I remember is trying to move, and I couldn't. It's like I was paralyzed…[the doctors] said I was about two hours from dying."

Eminem checked himself out of the hospital but was readmitted almost immediately when he overdosed again. Once he got out of the hospital, he hired a personal drug counselor who helped him get clean. "I'm looking at my kids and [realizing], 'I need to be here for this,'" he said in the documentary *How to Make Money Selling Drugs*.

By 2009, Eminem was clean and sober and ready to dive back into his first love: music. That May, he

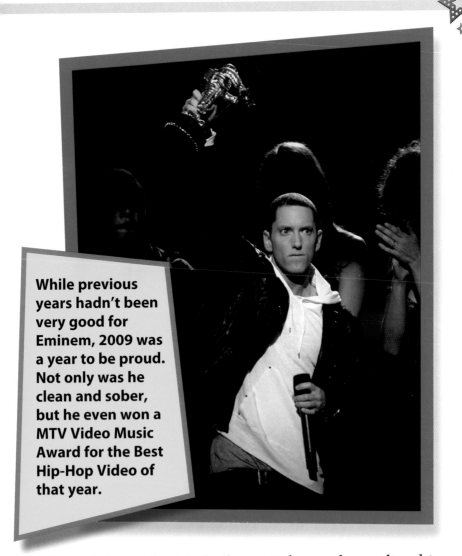

While previous years hadn't been very good for Eminem, 2009 was a year to be proud. Not only was he clean and sober, but he even won a MTV Video Music Award for the Best Hip-Hop Video of that year.

released the aptly titled album, *Relapse,* chronicling his recent experiences with drugs. Featuring hit singles such as "We Made You," "3 a.m.," and "Beautiful," *Relapse* debuted as the top album in America, selling 600,000 copies in a week. Those sales numbers were nowhere near what Eminem's earlier releases had achieved. But critics and fans still considered the album a success, especially considering what its creator had gone through

At the 2010 Grammy Awards, Eminem performed with other hip-hop superstars, Drake (left) and Lil Wayne (right).

to get to that point. In 2010, Eminem released a more introspective follow-up to *Relapse*. He called it *Recovery*, and it also debuted as the top-selling album in the country.

Recovery helped Eminem set a Guinness World Record as the top-selling album act in the twenty-first century with 32,241,000 units sold. Eminem also holds the world record for "Most Successive U.S. No. 1 Albums by a Solo Artist," and "Most Successive U.S. Albums to Debut at No. 1 by a Solo Artist." He also once held the record for most "likes" of a Facebook page with 42.5 million (by March 2014, his page had 84 million "likes"), and in 2011 he became the first U.S. artist to reach one billion views on YouTube.

Eminem decided to bring his career somewhat full circle with the 2013 release of *The Marshall Mathers LP 2*. By titling it as a sequel to what many believed to be his best album to date, *The Marshall Mathers LP*, the pressure was on the rapper.

Though he downplayed the fact that the album was a sequel to his 21-million-selling 2000 effort, Eminem did admit to working as hard as he had in a long time on *The Marshall Mathers LP 2*. He told *Rolling Stone*:

Chapter 6

"Rap God"

Before Eminem and Rihanna collaborated on the hit song "The Monster," they had another popular song together called "Love the Way You Lie."

"Calling it *The Marshall Mathers LP 2*, obviously I knew that there might be certain expectations. I wouldn't want to call it that just for the sake of calling it that. I had to make sure that I had the right songs—and just when you think you got it, you listen and you're like…I feel like it needs this or that,' to paint the whole picture."

The Marshall Mathers LP 2 had this and that—at least fans believed it did. When the album was released in November, it sold 792,000 copies in the first week. Eminem had strategically released four singles from the album—almost back to back—prior to the release of the album. The singles included "Berzerk," "Survival," "Rap God," and "The Monster," a dark and emotional collaboration with Barbadian singer Rihanna. The pair had teamed up on record a few times previously, including on the 2010 number-one hit, "Love the Way You Lie."

Although *The Marshall Mathers LP 2* was calmer than many of its predecessors, it still brought about its share of controversy. The lyrics to "Rap God," for example, contained the disparaging words "fag," "fags," and "faggots." Eminem's use of those words—just as it had a decade earlier—angered many openly gay musicians. Some critics, too, believed that by presenting lyrics similar to those he had written years earlier, Eminem had shown he had not matured much in his forty-one years on earth. *The Wall Street Journal* wrote: "Fortunately, the world has moved on, even if Eminem hasn't. He may have a specific person in mind with his

[derogatory lyrics]. So what? It's still childish. I don't really care if Eminem is or isn't a homophobe. I just wish he'd stopped being so lazy and find some other punching bag besides the LGBT community."

Although it may appear that way to some, it is unlikely that laziness had much to do with Eminem's decision to rap anti-gay slurs on his latest album. Over the years, Eminem has become a shrewd businessman, one who knows that controversy sells. People were talking about *The Marshall Mathers LP 2* weeks before it was released. Musical trends had changed in the years since Eminem first burst onto the scene, but newspapers and magazines still were writing about him. His music was selling in large numbers. People still knew his name.

"The entire industry has changed, and I have no idea where it's going," Eminem wrote in his 2008 autobiography. "People are always going to want music—no, they're always going to need music. Which means there will always be a place for me in this game.… If I had to do it again, I don't know if I would. I'm glad, though, that my music has brought people together."

Discography

Infinite, 1996

The Slim Shady EP, 1997

The Slim Shady LP, 1999

The Marshall Mathers LP, 2000

Devil's Night (with D12), 2001

The Eminem Show, 2002

D12 World (with D12), 2004

Encore, 2004

Relapse, 2009

Recovery, 2010

Hell: The Sequel (with Bad Meets Evil), 2011

The Marshall Mathers LP 2, 2013

Internet Addresses

OFFICIAL WEB SITE
www.eminem.com
OFFICIAL TWITTER PAGE
www.twitter.com/eminem

Selected Honors and Awards

1999   Best New Artist, MTV Video Music Awards

2000   Best Rap Solo Performance, Grammy Awards
Best Rap Album, Grammy Awards
Best Male Video, MTV Video Music Awards
Best Rap Video, MTV Video Music Awards
Video of the Year, MTV Video Music Awards
Lyricist of the Year, *Source* Awards
Music Video of the Year, *Source* Awards

2001   Best Rap Album, Grammy Awards
Best Rap Performance by a Duo or Group
(with Dr. Dre), Grammy Awards
Best Rap Solo Performance, Grammy Awards
Video of the Year, *Source* Awards

2002   Video of the Year, MTV Video Music Awards
Best Male Video, MTV Video Music Awards
Best Rap Video, MTV Video Music Awards

2003   Best Music, Original Song, Academy Awards
Best Rap Album, Grammy Awards
Best Music Video, Short Form, Grammy
Awards

Best Video from a Film, MTV Video Music Awards

2004 Best Rap Solo Performance-Male, Grammy Awards

Best Rap Song, Grammy Awards

2009 Best Hip-Hop Video, MTV Video Music Awards

2010 Best Rap Performance by a Duo or Group (with Dr. Dre and 50 Cent), Grammy Awards

Best Rap Album, Grammy Awards

Best Male Video, MTV Video Music Awards

Best Hip-Hop Video, MTV Video Music Awards

2011 Top Rap Album, *Billboard* Music Awards

Top Billboard 200 Album, *Billboard* Music Awards

Top Male Artist, *Billboard* Music Awards

Top Rap Artist, *Billboard* Music Awards

Top Rap Song (with Rihanna), *Billboard* Music Awards

Best Rap Album, Grammy Awards

Best Rap Solo Performance, Grammy Awards

2013 Artist of the Year, YouTube Music Awards

Index

48